Like Flaming Fields
Stoked by a Gentle Breeze

Like Flaming Fields Stoked by a Gentle Breeze:

One Woman's Sojourn from Pain

Sarah L. Brinklow

Writers Club Press

San Jose New York Lincoln Shanghai

Like Flaming Fields Stoked by a Gentle Breeze:
One Woman's Sojourn from Pain

Writers Club Press
an imprint of iUniverse, Inc.

For information address:
iUniverse, Inc.
5220 S. 16th St., Suite 200
Lincoln, NE 68512
www.iuniverse.com

ISBN: 0-595-22041-X

Printed in the United States of America

This collection of poetry is dedicated to my children, John Jesse and Casey Lynn, who, though they may not be ready to receive it or grasp it all, deserve my thanks and all the Love in the World. John and Casey, you are collectively my Rock. Love you.....Mama

Contents

Foreword

I have been many places in this life and, I think, before. I have loved, and lost. What I hope to generate with this collection of poems of the last 25 years, is the strength of a soul reaching out to the reader, hoping that that common affinity will take wings in your heart and soar, that pain is a daily occurrence in life, as is love, and it will, oddly enough, enrich us and strengthen us.

Acknowledgements

For my parents, Rosemarie (the teacher) and Gerald Brinklow, who reiterated the importance of an education.

Chapter One: Love

Martyr

in as much as i trust you, i fear you
for disregarding your gentle nature, you
are still a man of power
and in my eyes power signifies pain
a certain pain i hope to
never see again
Because a stern talking to
or a word can make me feel put in my place
misunderstood, shamed and stripped for the
whole human race
at the same time a fear rises up in my throat
that cuts off my wind, makes me grab for my
        coat
to run out of this house, known as you and me
terrified of again living trapped in the misery,
        not seeing
the door through the smoke pouring out of your
        ears
and the flames in your eyes wanna kill me
Doesn't matter if you would never put your
        hands on me
found out long ago that words punched me in
        the gut much
much harder
once again i can be no man's Martyr

Warning Shots

Should i take these inklings as warning shots
fired from that testosterone gun trapping me
helpless wounded lying on the ground
face slammed hard into the ground
Under the foot of an oppressor?

Ah the men in my life who have oppressed me
        the most
haven't done it solely on slaps and bruises
but in their words and their hurting deceiving
        witholding, the
Emotional stalemate
we came to each time, afraid to admit the
        volatility
of a love much like ours, oil and water, fade to
        black
each time i would hit the ground knocked
        unconscious
victim of a mind-maiming brain screw
A warning shot fired over the heads in
a hell suite for two?

Flattery

Although you may flatter me
With preludes sweet, and
lilac winds may blow through your hair,
the thought of your eyes meeting mine again has
captivated me once more.
for roses and wine would not be enough
if I were able to bathe you in them slowly
by candlelight
Tasting you as I go.

Untitled

All my love is for you
Every breath I take
I hold deep
inside me
thinking of your kiss, holding you oh, so close
Your hands moving precisely over me like they
      were designed for this specific purpose

Being without you, love, it hurts to be apart, for
you alone hold the keys to my heart,
Your love, I
hold so deep
Inside me
thinking of your sighs, your size
Moving through me, where it craves to be

Answer me
when I cannot speak
Call to me
When i cannot hear
Make me hear, hear so deep
when you call on me, I will draw strength

Make love to me with your thoughts
Heal me with your words
Kisses of love, let them rain on me,
Reign in my soul, you do
Comfort me, so deep
Let me hold you tonight with my promise

that I am yours and no others'

I crave you tonight, my love
and all that awaits
We will be together I know
this
as your word is like rock
And oh so deep into the rock
Our love forged with metal alloy
melded together
Holds that promise

TIME.

why, Time?
Wait, making me wait, driving me
    to
Desire you like
    no other?

filling the time. i turn to driftwood
if I try hard enough it can be done
But the longing, oh the longing
So desperately longing for a touch, a sapphire-laden
phrase
diamond-eyed glances
mahogany caresses, so smooth and decadent

lost Soul
cry out to my heart
bleed for me
are you on your way
Sing your song to me, fill me with a presence
Look to me, cause me to turn my head away,
Overcome
with a vision

Adrift on that English blue Channel called your
    eyes.

With One Look at You

With one look at you,
the world became awash with
colours and musical air
    the pond grew still and I
felt the need to walk
on it just to have one
look at you———-

With one look at you,
My heart became molten
and all the beating and sweating with desire
One love One heart
So many needs fulfilled
With one look at you———-

Shove It Up Your Ass

You can shove it up your ass
As far as it can go
Take it
You WILL take it
For all the lies you told

BOUND

Powder blue beacons of pale would shine up at me
        each time I took you
lying in helpless surrender, hands fastened ever so
Tightly above your head, Breathless
Anticipatory longings
of a Soul caught in a Paradox
of a Need
to be Owned, that was oddly enough Unattainable
A desperate Being longing to be
Set Free
Bound to Self.

Enter me with your eyes

Enter me with your eyes
Tease me with your smiles
Feed me with your lips, so sweet
Shower me with rain so warm and pungent
Melting me

Give me the chance, oh so willing
to lower my soul down on you
Grinding it down
leaving you lying, breathless beneath
A kind of
Surrender
Beyond your control

Hands pressed
Above your head
In a submission known only by a Queen and her
Concubine
A dance danced for two

Bedazzled

All the trappings of a day for two
Brilliant sun, blossoming trees, but no you
Want to embrace the sun but I find it hard
Splintered Longings in my eye like a shard

Willing your kisses, open wide....
Traces of you still deep inside
Light on the blooms, a testament to you
Confirming this ache, love, you know I do

Counting the moments till I hold you tight
Breathless, wonderful sleep into night
Falling like the bloom petals, like a spring snow
Knowing so deep one blessed day soon we'll
        never let go

A Plea Resigned

Come away with me
Give way, Allow your soul to be
Free, Arrest the cobwebs that flay in your head
Whisper at them, send them off to bed.

Tribunal trying Tainted love at your hand
Decries allegations
of a misanthropic Maid
gone Screwy,
Deflect Reject
The Dilemma
at hand, an unjustly accused, hot sparks,
     Reeling, Feeling,
   Pain.

Measured Indifference

Fire away, moon me with a careless rant,
Romp on through the new life you've spawned
Fueled by parasitic energy drained from me by
     you
With the upmost in indifference

You who watched the kids while she acquired
     academic enlightenment
(Thoroughly resenting every microsecond of
     that charity)
Has now managed to somehow exploit the
     kindnesses of This woman
Unbeknownst to her,
Stripper of souls upward by arrogant mobility.

Park me in the garage of that Brady Bunch, Split
     level American dream of your mind. I will
     make it in the illusion you've placed me in,
     knowing fully well that that vision doesn't
     portend to me.

Milk Carton

So off you went to e
        va
            por
                ate
get it straight, it Is real
not "Was"; to
Deny this, a
Travesty, nowhere bound, nowhere
found
Faceless memory at 2%.

Looking for you
on the carton in my mind beside the
Breakfast cereal
While reading Personals
(not the funnies at all)
….Lost, strayed….if found, please
Return to…….
        Reward!!!

Misled

Where do I find my soul, now
that you have mislaid it?
Not far from a precipice
teetering on an edge?

Spent lives lie carelessly wasted
a product of a dream never manifested
Can you hear the sound of the rain
in the trees?
Proudly, back turned, watching me, as the rain
pours down my cheeks,
Era of a love I seek
Gone by at your discretion.
Could you look in my direction
and watch me bleed….I cannot see how?

Serpentine Rail

Diamondback, you slither away
into your own narrow opening
Writhing, reeling in your own emotional pain
Driven by a sense of urgency unsurpassed,
      runaway train, and Me,
Tied to the tracks of your soul, barreling over
      me
you metamorphose once more, changeable,
      charlatan, chameleon, You now
None of those things you ever were, your Love
      for me, a Ruse, entirely, it Seems.

My heart is a graveyard wherein lies our Union
      of love, sweet cherry blossoms
Fallen,
Blanketing the graves
Copious are the tears that fall rapidly from a
      quickly changing sky, a testimony to
A love
Gone by——————
As the Serpentine railroad winds on....

Us, the Magical Reality

Well could I
i don't think?
Acquire you elsewhere?
See, from where I am sitting, the search,
futile,
would lean violently to the Left, a distinct
Impossibility
The Magical Reality we Are.

So Catch me, or watch me fall.
You never knew how tightly I would hold you
while tending your Heart.
Edifying, self-defying leaps of faith
Propping and stoking a fragile countenance,
my Sweet Sun Baby, your only crime a
Heart of Glass.

We built a monument to our love.
A brightly coloured lighthouse of multi-paned
Cathedral Glass
The dimming light still glowing within
But with sandbags piled ever so highly and
        plainly,
And as much as I drench your soul
You've blocked the Spindrift from crashing into
        your eroded
shore once more, as it has so many times before
Not allowing yourself, eyes shut, awash in my
        mist

Like Flaming Fields Stoked by a Gentle Breeze

In a crippling self-imposed mindfreeze
like
Cryogenic denial
Awaiting a thaw.

sb/sb 2001

miss you

Sarah L. Brinklow

Trailer Trash Meets Lovelorn Lost

Trailer Trash and
Lovelorn Lost, hobbling
through Life, as though
idiosyncrasies
Were a crime, designed
to set you Off.

You loved my quirky
wicked ways, nothing else could
heighten you.

Snare if capture, lovelorn,
weak and powerless
Frantic mindmeld-mindwrestle, catching
a snag on your
spintered heart?

Could you not see how it could bludgeon
that remained?
Inner workings, dashed and bent,
like a timepiece dropped from a hundred-story
building.
Take us apart, loosen the gears within, slow to
Numb Steel.

Silent Grief

Welcome silent
death of my soul,
Come, close my coffin lid with a bang
for all that once was once eternal is Now no
      more.
We both knew Salvation would only come but
      once for us, and after that
Love would not exist again in that way for the
      two little dead children.
(a siamese surgical separation).
No chance of survival without sharing the same
      vital organs

Turn the key on the lock, for You have sealed the
      lid
Lowered the box into the ground.
It was said that you would not be among
the wailing mourners who would throw
      themselves
into that hole known as Us
Demonstrative of some sole-serving move to
      save Self.

The Test

When you put the foreign coins into my hand
we shared a look and you spurred me on
Across the hollow street to the bakery shop
where I would see if I could "cut it"
make a purchase of a loaf with a casual air

I trembled with excitement at the test, felt i
     could prove
some sort of self worth as your english bride
to pass this test would be a milestone for me, i
     trembled
shutting the gate behind me, you, nodding,
urging me on

Crossing the street, would I ever reconcile the
     thought in my
mind, of cars catapulting the on the wrong side?
i felt like your little girl as you watched me,
     smiling from that window

i did it! the woman with the accent grinned and
     didn't ask!
Did I pass? I thought of it at the time as a
     surreptitious rite of
passage. I triumphantly returned with our
     treasure, the kind of
simple joy we'd hoped to share each day for The
     rest of our lives.
Breathless sigh....we were going to be together!!!

Didn't I cut it with you? didn't i pass? why am i a
    little girl all
alone in the street, locked out of the gate? i
    thought you loved me?

Echoes from the Wishing Well

It's as if the well has run dry
The clock's hands have ceased movement
The stars are set, frozen in the winter sky
The phone lies silent, there where it always has.
For today, a kind of love found nowhere on
       earth
Lost its spark.

All the streetlights lost their glow tonight
Christmas trees all lit, fade to black
No real desires to deck any halls this year
For the Love I had has turned away from my
       heart,
Brought me no real solace on this blue spinning
       sphere, only heartbreak

A penance once more has had to be paid, the
       price for my loving
at someone's outstretched expense
For now your words are clenched and striking
They hit so hard, with your poised indifference.

Bruising an anesthetized inner core,
your bashing and pummeling , confounding all
       Reason
for "Why should I Be if you won't be with me?"
is the cry to you

from the tiny frightened girl at the bottom of
      the well
of wishes

And the echoes will chill you, maybe even kill
      you, Still
Turn on a dime and be gone
For the lights went out on my Life tonight

Something that one whom i gave my heart to
      never even cared to know.

That Cobalt Dream Never Made Realized

all i ever wanted in my life
was to spend it with a man like you
we always wanted it the same
someone who respected us, appreciated us,
One
melded into the other,
That Cobalt Blue Dream Never Made Realized.

well, Somewhere between fantasy and reality,
        reality got mislaid
and cold cruel reality took hold
and the world became a hostile place
my nationality a shame
a prisoner, political, left on my own shore

i could have sworn we transcended it all
One implicitly comprehending the other
always working it through, instinctively sensing
        the other's heart
Never like all those who came before to wound
        us both
Trust tempered with an understanding.

how you could even fathom
that we no longer needed one another or that it
        wasn't worth the pain
i refuse to believe
set me down on hot coals, would you

you might as well have ripped out my arteries
and let the lifeblood drain for what's left of me
your little girl who waits still for you, your
      mistress, your Love.

So when u set down my thoughts tonight,
go to sleep and turn out the light with a moan,
my name still on your lips in spite of time
      passed,
i would like to know how You can bear it,
for i cannot

and when you awake in the morning sun, sleep
      still in your eyes
all that I would want from you would be this:
to look into that mirror you once watched us in
and see the eyes of a man i once knew
who would never, ever, couldn't bear to hurt me
and tell that man he is untrue

may your reflection turn away in shame
at the very sight of you.

For the heart that waits for you who always
      waited for you
Still holds you so tightly, refusing this lie
how a heart like yours can look away from that
      kind of a love is colder than the coldest
      Lake Ontario day
Cobalt blue, our souls etched there at your own
      hand that day
a promise that just won't go away

The Moors

The descent from the air upon the Moors
was to be the closest I would ever get to them.
As we wafted and taxied in dreamy insolence,
the silence caused by the pressure in one's ears
created a vacuum-like state.
For this was as close to heaven as I would ever find
*   myself,*
drifting down off of a cloud to you,
halfway between heaven and hell.

Just Ask Me

So go on then, ask me, would I much rather
be a part of you,
Laying and writing before me on a bed of
     agony?
A constant for you with the love we were in
When the manic, sadomasochistic mind that
     was you
Residing in that prison of pain (from which you
     both sought release
and found it—
through the medium of slitting my airway)
     would take hold

The answer, my lover, may both surprise and
     astound
when you realize
that with your freedom came a
noose for my neck
For something inside of me has died.

How I can still feel for a love you deny
Perpetuates all of the pain inside
And it won't go away.
None of it will
The problem you see, was that I cared for you
     still

raw

once again i found myself wanting to speak
to the one i loved more than no other
wanting to speak from my heart and my soul
as i thought you knew i had before
i ache and i bleed and i'm raw

i'm just keep trying to find the right words that
      will wake you
from that sleep that i know will just hurt, wanna
      shake you
but you just can't seem to hear me, you don't
      want to see me
from the sound of it, it seems you can no longer
      feel me
Someone deliver me from this heartache i feel
I bleed and I ache and goddamn it its real
see i cant forget us and i'm raw

our lives,separated
so an alien a concept to me
My God, this was never supposed to have
      happened
Your heart and mine, interwined
Seems you've put me out of sight
but can you keep me out of mind?
the ache in my head is the ache in my heart
the longing i have that we'd never ever part
my spirit it aches and i'm raw.

i started to drive to the lake the other day
a stark winter's day, volatile, changeable
the sky driving that way a pewter grey black
but the whiteout by the church turned me back
wanted So to stand In those wide white Spa-ces
     you knew
Scream at the Top of my Lungs that it wasn't
     fucking true
till it reached the other shore
that i just cant take it anymore
as a life without you,
     Stevie,
it just wasnt supposed to happen.
i could never accept it just as
you could never have kept walking
my body aches and it bleeds and i'm raw.

But you did and i have and it hurts and the pain
keeps on reeling, dont think
i can ever be the same i dont love i cant heal my
     mind its in tatters
my heart. like crushed glass grinding under car tires
ground to fine powder
into my soul's very core
Save me, Someone
from my grief!
Splintered glass in my eye I cant see anymore
I bleed
i ache
it's not gonna end didn't u care enough that it
     would come to this for us
like an open, gaping wound
i'm raw

An Englishman's Eyes Were My Demise

while trying to analyze this pull they have on me
i thought of your smile
how your whole face would light up like a little
    child
and you would blush and look down at your
    hands
much like my daughter when she was small
those lucid Bombay Sapphires
that with a look, could set my existence
    smoldering

you loved me
those eyes didn't lie
the only time i couldn't trust them
was in the avoidance when i watched the wheels
    turn, coping skills
gone awry
in a pristine Lancashire country sky

love me, never leave me
my angel you were true
till something ugly took hold of you
and i then lost my control, my spell on you
the pieces in the puzzle then fit

For the hideousness inside your head
made you think that you'd be better dead
or was it me you envisioned lying there

when i took your place there stepped off that
    chair
Your hands and yours alone
that gave the chair that final pull?
I closed my eyes and saw your pretty eyes before
    me that day
as you draped that hangman's noose
around my heart that night on the phone
for it was there i was left
abandoned once more ,
left to live it all out alone
the sin of love my only crime
read at my hanging
Only the crowd jeered
and walked away at this execution
And you were at the front
counting the minutes till i breathed my last
you had a train to catch and you were late

Sarah L. Brinklow

Turning that Corner Back

You still seemed to pride yourself on this fact:
that you always could walk away and come back
well why bother gloating when this time
You won't

you told me one of the times with fear in your
voice
that an Us so volatile would always
be just that
so good for a time and then off you would walk
your major concern that you would not return

For With every episodic hump
Up the rollercoaster ride of that beautiful mind
I exhaustively prided myself on bringing you back
Crunched in a ball, drained of life while you made
your
Ascent

Ah, abject fear, a light goes on!!
i'm starting to see it was you, again, not me
not enough faith in yourself that you could stay
no, you see,
it would Never be me
who thought you could walk
Away and not turn that corner back.

Too Deep

Remember the tree, love, remember the tree
that crisp cobalt March day, so brilliant the sky
when you painstakingly carved those mirrored
      initials in the bark
and we thought our love would never die

well baby its been nearly a year now
and that time of year is here,
once again I'm back to the tree where I ran all
      last year
running my hands over the bark, wishing you
      back here

didn't want to hurt it so i tried the other day
don't ask me how, i didn't cry
coarse sandpaper in my pockets, brave little one
      in tow
Knew in her heart that it had to go
told her that someday you'd go on a trip
would search for days and not find me or it

Rubbed and ground it to our exasperation
she looked up to me remarking i was making a
      funny face,
trying to fix me, as i scrunched up my nose
      much as someone with an ax wielding it
      behind them to make blows
the pain when it didn't work, nobody knows....

A tear in her eye and a deep baby sigh
not knowing why or how to fix me
I sighed back as I ground the hard bark, praying
      please Someone release me
Till I wiped the powder away, simply shaking my
      head saying,
Honey, it won't go away….it's just too deep….

night chills

On a night when cold,
crisp air fills the room
the window, open a crack
in your February tomb
Remember me, and
know that I am
with you

with those words, sighed so breathlessly,
crying please, please honey, come back to me
knowing the loss, oh so all alone
clutching the silent evil phone, that
enemy, how can it be, when it once brought you so
close to me?

Sarah L. Brinklow

THE DAY OF
REMEMBERING

When I remembered the cobalt dream
late last night while shuffling through papers
it hit me today would be the day
of Remembering

it was a year ago today
that we met
A snowy night waited out for you
at the Rochester airport

Can't even bring myself now to think
of the happiness we held that night
Holding each other in lost baggage claim
the world became ours as in your eyes i saw stars

It snowed last night but it was not the same
i fell off to sleep alone this time with no
stellar future plans for two
for all i really ever wanted in life was to be with
        you
and as its no more there's not a lot i can do

Oddly enough, this week the sun shines that
        same Bright
as geese in flight, chanting hello or is it goodbye
fly back to that lake that we found so
        accomodating

that seemed to hold us together, that and a tree
    carved deeply
when we found ourselves quaking
Only this time it's Me here left shaking

and the March Ontario sun
calls to me in all her blinding brilliance
intensifying my aloneness
conceding it may be permanent
Announcing that it was a long time ago
and is no more
and i stand solo on this shore
Goddammit
Once More.

For this Day of Remembering can only remind
that Forever is a long, long time
and True Love was just a State of Mind

ANNIVERSARY

you don't want to know how I'm feeling
situation's spun out of control
humiliation, degradation
robs the heart and now the soul
Curiousity killed me
but first it killed the cat
Opportunity's lost me
i couldn't tell you where I'm at

So don't shove it in my face
when you go and find another
never wanted it that way
to hear all about your lover,
Still to live a life without you,
devoid of what we had
seems oh so fucking wrong to me
and I'm just so goddamned sad

It's been so long now
seems like our distant past
till someone asks about us
and then the thoughts come bolting, fast
and then panic, how it hurts
to think of a love cut down, so true,
i just can't bear to do all this
without a man like you

The City of London Welcomes You

"I WAS A GIRL, NOW I'm a boy….call 01923
    191 696"
Red phone booths full of adverts
Of perverts
They rip them down twice a day
And they're back the next

Lying in the doorways, can't get too close
Homeless, forgotten, their stench is carried into
        the street
Wrapped up in blankets, sleeping in daylight
People milling around them, the homeless, the
        nameless, the
Oblivious.

Walking the winding path in St. James Park
Gazing at the pond leading to the palace of the
        Queen
One would wonder if a swan sale wouldn't be in
        order
Maybe then They wouldn't be lying there,
Rotting
Just a street away?

Sarah L. Brinklow

Cream Crackers and Bovril

Cream crackers and Bovril
Became my obsession
When I left you at that gate
Your world became my own

Standing in your mother's kitchen. my arms
      wrapped around you
As you cooked for me
Spreading Bovril
While waiting for tea

British Rail Out of London

Tired from running
We hit the Underground
Relieved to find a seat this time
As the train pulled out.

Eyes rolling back in my head
Lulled into a dream state
Head on your shoulder as rowhouses, then trees
Flew past. Nothing like it,
British Rail.

Contented travellers, you and I
We said nothing, we didn't have to
Glances from others proved what we felt
Wrinkled matron grinned with a tear in her eye

From behind, a voice
Brought us to life
A homemade triangle case came off his back.
"I'D LIKE TO PLAY YUH A TUNE, A
        SCOTTISH MELODY DOES ANYONE
OBJECT, SAY NOW!"

He tapped his feet and played
I felt like a true Celt
My head grew dizzy with the reel
Travellers were smiling to themselves
As we transcended the mundane

Looking at you with question
For it was like no Amtrak trip I'd known
I pondered the magic of it all
And chalked it up to..a
Little bit of British Rail
And a lot of
You.

Untitled

and there you were
a beam of light, your
eyes ablaze like
the sun against an azure sky
pulling me toward you

DOUBLE BETRAYAL

Nervously, I
fed my pain
cold rain falling
forecast of the eminent chill.
A betrayal.

Food, you tried to
fill my need
The Comfort Quotient, how I
needed you
to intercede, then completely
Deny you—
in my grief.

Damn you both.
Betrayer of passion
Denier of my own worth.

WRITING FROM AN ACHE

Writing from an ache
I seek to repair my broken heart, you
left me in pieces, You, the only love I
ever knew
To save yourself
　　You denied me, to save
　　me, you turned away, choosing instead a
　　life other than that which we'd planned, a
　　Life devoid of our passion.

　　Real it was
　　You can't take that away from me
　　Can't deny your love, nor my love that I held
　　you
　　　Abandoned
　　　Left crushed and matted into the
　　　carpet of our eternities

　　　Turning your back
　　　Not looking back
　　　Walking away
　　　Should never have let you gone away
　　　Why didn't you stay?

Chapter Two: Indifference

EXISTENCE

I can feel summer
ripening to fruition
Intense and full
everything is green and ample
just on the brink of
dying, freezing
trapping me inside
alone
      lonelier than even
a summer could be
with two striking children trying to
be happy and the family from hell
"Making the best of it"
trudging through life,
sort of
existing through life?

NOTHING

There is nothing in me that can love you
      anymore
Anyone who has this little regard for me I
      cannot love
Ten years ago " 'they' say I made a mistake
you make "them" right everytime.
You'd treat a stranger better than me.
You'd take no from anyone but me.
You treat me like a dirty old rug;
you keep wiping your feet…over and over and
      over again.
Ten years ago I thought my love for you
could rise above your misguided soul
and that we could be there for each other.
But with each lie
and push
and demand
you've pushed me further away to the point
where we just live in the same dwelling;
but you seem to call me property
in everything you ask.
There is no love here; only a
pitiful man,
a broken woman, a lost love and
two babies caught in the middle.
Maybe the best present I could get
for this 10th anniversary
we can never attain.
Maybe the only gift you could give

would be…either a real promise
built on real action or a
permanent solution.
It defies my spirit that
a human being could care so very little
for their wife.
Such callous disregard
for another.

a marriage in twilight

So many nights, I wish I
felt safe with you
Felt love from you
Could trust in you

So many days I've not expected a thing of you
Been emotionally drained by you
Been trampled and dumped
by you
    So many years, I watched go by with you
Never a
care from you
Always a
prayer for you
Learned how to die
from you

Spindrift

Pain rushes
    in like waves
      beating down the shoreline
       it erodes and quakes
       with the persistence
Of the tide in your eyes

Guilt

The ragged edge
that was tucked underneath,
oppressed and forgotten
But when emerged, it becomes
the sharpened sword, the
eating away of the soul, the
obstacle that never fades. Its
claws grip; its fangs impale me
on the fences of hell, ripping
at me, and I bleed...
Boiling droplets that rust the fiery
fences I am impaled upon!
Sin and fallen angels are our fallen fences;
and bitter tears fall down upon the sidewalk
of life in confusion and shame.

a twilight of pain

in the twilight
that no one can see
There I stand
in the shadows
watching the river run
There i speak to you,
    aloud
hoping you will hear
But you turn away

In the twilight
That everyone will see
There I dance
on the clouds
running the sea to its shore
It's there that I sing to you, quite
loudly,
Knowing you will hear
Yet you ignore me

In the sunlight
Where we alone shall see
There we will sit
in fields of tall grass
and poppies
by a whispering brook feeding you sunkisses
There i strum on my guitar and sing you sad
    songs,
softly

You can't help but hear——-
And you yawn and look at your watch.

    *   *   *   *   *   *   *   *   *   *

Sketches of unfulfilled longings——-I don't know
    what they mean anymore——-than anyone
    else does!!! My emotions, someone else's
    stories.

Sarah L. Brinklow

True Strength in Will

I look up to the skies
from whence cometh my help
smoke pours and glass shatters
bright flames against a December sky,
blackened by night's twisted hands.
Beloved friends are brought down
frightened, shaken, bloodied. Just another
      obstacle in their race
to the finish
Why, Jesus,
    WHY?
Just how much pain can an individual
undertake in a lifetime?
Knarled and wrinkled, they sit and wait, what
      can come next in these
Wise, passing lives? How can something
so Very Fragile withstand such constant pain?

The strength of a soul endures life
and lives it in the fullest sense of the word....

That I might be so strong as these!

Sometimes I wonder....

....Sometimes
When life goes by so fast that I
cannot ever grasp hold of him—-
....Sometimes

     *   *   *   *   *

Do you know why I cry?
I cry....sometimes. When I'm alone and you
        can't see me—
when I'm with pain and sorrow greets me
When I can't see your eyes anymore
because you never once
stopped to look at mine...

Darkness

Loads of Love
flows from such deep
wounds
onto those who
have been chosen
to become a part of a whole
and then say no
and retreat into these wounds; they fester,
they bellow, they cry out, reaping darkness'
      rewards
Darkness is a rejected heart,
and a festering wound is its legacy.

Speculation

I wonder where you might be
now, and what you might think about
El Salvador, "no nukes"
the winter's thaw
If spring will ever come to this cold, old valley,
        and why
are we all here on this same planet, spinning all
        around,
sparking Green
like Lifesavers chewed in the dark.

And I wonder how we hold the strength to wait,
        or does someone
hold it for
us?
and what do you do with your time
while I mull over mine
as though it were a ball and chain?

Sarah L. Brinklow

Gentle, Sensitive

Gentle, sensitive
it always has to be there
but everytime, its different
I always want to grasp it
in a hurry. But the more I
yearn, the more quickly
it slips from my hands.

Still Life

the world this day
    is a
      "still life".
Rain waits patiently
      in the powder gray
         heights of the sky
In eager anticipation
      of cascading down to meet the earth.

my life this day
is a "still life"
Tears abide quietly
in the
deep-brown
depths of my eyes
In eager anticipation
      of your return,
         '77

On Loss

A wide, gaping mouth—
Its rim smeared in "Cadillac Red"
(Red-tag special-only 89 cents, she beams)
Two tired eyes
that tell a story—
one of love one, of hate, of bitterness,
      resentment;
of sadness.
Teased tousled, as was her heart,
curls of platinum blond stand
(under the auspices of Final Net).
Dangle earrings rock in precision with her
      rhythmic
gum chewing.
Poured into a windbreaker -not her own- a
worn emblem exclaims "Union Hill Fire
      Department."
(She wears that part over her heart.)
He used to drape it over her once-frail
      shoulders
on crisp fall evenings when they went up to the
firehouse to play cards
Her plump, calloused hands clutch at her food
      stamps
She still wears her ring
(She insists each week at the beauty parlor that it
aids in fighting off all the men).
As she tosses her usual two packs of Luckies
      onto the

belt, I notice
her kid under the cart who
stops reading the back of the Cheerios box.
(Free "Star Wars" lasergun)
He silently pulls at the leg of
her hot pink stretch pants
and stares innocently up at her
His big blue eyes ablaze, he asks—
"Mommy, when did you say my daddy was
        coming
back?"

Sarah L. Brinklow

The Rain Has Come

the rain has come
an anticipated torrent
of cold, splashing droplets,
sent once more
to cool the earth.
And you will return,
an anticipated burst
of loving, warming rays of sunshine
sent once more
to warm my soul.

a sense of self?

Am I that person I see staring back at me
From the bottom of my mug?
Or is the person within
someone who I've never seen
before?

Often when the fruits of my assertion
come splashing back at me
the makeup cakes and creases in the tears, and
the friends aren't laughing anymore.

I wonder-
    who is that great eye
drowning in my glass
searching me for kind words and reassurances
only receiving silent looks of unknowing
in return?

Sarah L. Brinklow

Untitled

The rain beats down angrily in torrents
I'm afraid
the thunder crashes
much like the cymbals of a symphony,
—suddenly and without warning-
the lightning illuminates the earth
as if it were daylight

Now, a siren wails, so intense is its pain
Softly, growing
steadily louder
as the truck rushes by…

The old, gnarled tree has been
split in two
as a fire burns hungrily
out of control across town
….And the rain beats down,
angrily in torrents.

for what is life but a great Search?

*　　　　　*　　　　　*

we search for love
Seeking contentment in out lives
(if only for awhile)
we search for the Light
that we may escape the darkness

We seek darkness
the we might attempt to escape the light
But
Do our searches have endings?
DO they always even have meaning?
Meaning that can translate into logic?

Sarah L. Brinklow

A Child's Memory

They were black, sturdy shoes
Tight laces, short, sensible heels
Crinkled , worn leather at the toes
I found them in the closet at the old farmhouse
      that day when
I was nine
and I was full of knowing
that you had passed.

Sugarhigh

there is a time when all stands still
not much to be done for it, not always me to
     blame
yet i feel like a failure in everyone's eyes
assumptions are made, judgements rendered
isn't it bad enough that i feel the way that i do?
i would never judge you

Disease with a negative outcome
no matter how stringent the control
you've got me by the testicles, you do
it's win, lose or draw
for a life without you might be more enjoyable
a life never knowing your sacrifices and moods
     so much more
liveable
you see i hold a lot inside of me
when it comes to revealing your vices
for if i bared all and showed your face
still more would turn away, for
your face is ugly and cold, sad and lonely
hardly the warm and passionate woman that i
     know
but when i wear your mask
i may lose control

So i hide you i cloak you i minimize your
     existence
why stand out when no one wants to know?

if i play your cards close to my chest
Suck it in and say screw the rest
of you all who could really never understand
Maybe they will all continue to look the other
      way
And You won't hurt me quite so much
and I will become immune to your touch
until that dying day when
No one will come for me anyway.

So Glad I Never Knew What I Now Know

If I thought
for one second
that I would have had to suffer
the loneliness and pain
of raising two children to this age
alone
Isolated
Would I have ever continued on
in this sojourn?
Would I have pressed on past the pain
and the humiliation of a life of going without
....would I have struggled the way I have?

Or would I have waved the white flag
Stopped facing the music
Got off of the carousel
Or ridden away on the horse,
My getaway, on a collision course with insanity?
Let someone else take the reins with the express
        purpose, to dull my
pain?

Would they have been better off
If I had never chosen to take a stand
I don't believe that to be true
They say every child needs a dad
Something these two never had
I've been both for so long

Sarah L. Brinklow

Sometimes maybe its just not enough
To be the woman and the male
Example to a near man and a little girl craving
            love?

Chapter Three: People I Know and Love

Undying Devotion

as i sat at the pc
she scrunched herself up to a height of around
    three
a baby-young lady, caught in the middle
of dependence yet inde-pen-
-dent the little girl riddle
Looking right up at me, trust in her eyes
much like those days when she suckled and
    sighed
at me, as though I was all of her tinygirl world
i stopped working and smiled looked down at
    those
dark night sky eyes and asked her again, just like
    all
those times when i measured them, shouting
    Stop it!
and they'd squeal, delighted
said, Baby when you not gonna be able to fit
    under
this table no more
devoted eyes asserted
and Defiantly made a promise
of
Never.

Sweet Sweet Spirit, for Casey

Sweet, sweet Spirit, there's mischief
in those eyes
When you laugh so hard, no sound comes out,
Black eyes dancing, wisdom beyond years,
    beauty beyond mine,
Astounding

Song of a bird
floats on your breezes
Little angel girl with the fairies in her head
Dragging your man around dominantly, him
    powerless
the furry snowball, helpless to your charms
Lying in your arms

Baby darlin
you are sunshine to me
Warm wind and lovedrops spilling from the
    clouds
Arms around my neck, sticking to me like a
    postage stamp
Your mama's girl
Look out, world

Ramen Noodles

He has been reared on Ramen noodles
Compact rectangles of compressed ramen
Morning, noon and night, he would eat them
much to all their horror

Momma always said he was a picky eater,
the
    Saltier the better,
anythng zero nutrition was his demise
Affordable, embarassing, they became his all-
      purpose meal….
Ramens
$1.99 gets you a whole case at Tops
Life on this income makes this an attractive
      option

Ramen
Poverty
Comfort food for the masses.
Warm and salty.
Feed Us.

Man of Mama's House

Strong boy? No, Strong Man
You look at me, I cringe and smile
it's all different now with the deepening voice
and the nudge that can accidentally push me
     across a room
I stare, you say "What?" with your pubescent
     Apache look

Can't you see? Honey
I know you feel changes
that life rearranges
the best of us till it spins out of control

Testosterone surges breed threats from mom
of slapping estrogen patches on your ass in the
     night
Raising the voice, beating your chest
Still you respect me
you're really not like all the rest
And oh when I carried you
So safe and warm
and he could minimally affect you
though you saw him coming a mile away
as life was induced and you flew into my ribcage
     for cover

I knew you were overdue but under ready
for all the pain he threw on you
i hope i got you away from him in time

although the scars of the heart still burn
I didn't want to put it on you, honey we just
     found ourselves there
to see you three years later in post traumatic
     stress
how could I have put you in that mess

But you've proven your intensity and beauty
more loyal to me than the day is long
A man -boy boy-man
who can hold his head high
Reach for the sky honey
draw it and wear it
It's all yours now

Papa

He sits, as much
a part of his chair as
its arms and legs
of wood

In his pockets live
tiny screwdrivers, keys
and little brown Lincolns.
He cries, but he calls it
hayfever.

From every door and window
he watches me
as I pack for school
and talks of "getting a security job down there",
but...

....But he won't.
He'll stay in Penfield
and he'll see his children off
as they leap from the nest
with hurtful cries, tears
and freedom anew.
He will live here, die here,
and watch the birds fly southward,
their young brown wings
turning salt and pepper
in the dusk

As he flies, the wise, old wrinkled
eagle, to his home beyond the stars.
He will meet us and
the other smiling believers
and when he gets there,
watch him grin as he says, quite out of breath,
"I beat ya here like I said."

Woman of the Tradewinds

For my Mother

Raised as you were of a strong women, three
    sisters
a sperm donor long out the back door
i got a strong mother, unbeaten, hearty even
always rose to the challenge, would always take
    on more

but circumstance has dulled you, confidence has
    left
your side, you swim defeated, to the shore
and throw yourself up on the sand, crying stop it
    can't take it
anymore
a castaway engulfed in your own inner war

For the tradewinds that took you out to sea
cost you your soul, your symphony
the one you held inside your head
these days, you remark you'd be better off dead

As in the trade, the tradewinds took you off
    course
and you found yourself in that harbour called
    matrimony
an institution hellbent on draining the life out of
    many
lucky enough to survive that type of fate
the kind that i've received myself had to wait

to see if there was anything left in me
after the dicks left me crumpled in misery
in my own despair
while they bolted out the back once more

Seasons changed, the aggravation did not
though you begged to be cut Down from that
        Cross called a man
on you toiled till there was not much left
an empty ache inside
for the tradewinds had finally brought you a
        daddy that day
and a hurtful man a child bride.

A Good Man (one of the Last of a Good Breed)

For my Uncle, Frank Ugino

I tried to come to you
Just seemed my heart, it knew
Didn't try to hide
the Love
I held inside, for You'd suffered
For so long, Of all of us, just seemed so wrong
For you were kind, you were True
Just seemed your life was far from through

But the Pain, it just went on
Didn't seem there'd be an end
So it seemed only fair to you, sweet
Uncle, dear Friend
That it would be time to Ascend
Leaving us all to fend alone
Despite all your good,
Or was it due to it
Your destiny was sown?

As the gifts you imparted
Respect and dignity,
these two things have long since gone
From the minds of men
In harrowing times as these
When you come to me in my mind I recall
That in your eyes I saw

Quite a lot that went unsaid
No one ever knew just how much
it pained me so to reach you
that night when at the end of a phone
they called to tell me you were dead.

for Etta

In the quiet of the night
she walked in and sat down
upon my life
She didn't know that she could change it
Would rearrange it

Her smile
was the glistening of the sunshine
on the ocean's misty fingers, running
through her hair, streaks of moonlight
shining in her gentle eyes
Her laugh
was of a thousand silver bells
being pulled behind a sleigh
singing in the winter wind
"Lady Sings the Blues"
She would dance
like a little bird in flight
soaring, yet still struggling
crying in candlelight...
Maryetta...I can feel your pain
I can see your eyes
I hear them call my name
Maryetta....your daddy loves you so
Did you really know?

One morning, gentle woman, little bird you
soared into Abba's arms of love, His
strong, warm hands

now caress your face, so innocent
and wipe away my tears,
wiping mine away
His love
that you couldn't feel before
pulsates through you till
He becomes the new beat of your heart
His blood, yours now, running through your
        veins
Bandaging your broken wings He
Keeps you alive in the refuge
of His love, freckled little rose
and there, you sing
and there you soar
Lady sings the blues no more

Maryetta...I can feel your pain..
I can see your eyes
I hear them call my name
Maryetta..Abba loves you so
I believe that now, you know.
            '80

Awakening to You and Self

Englishman, yet native Son
your heart always on this shore, mine at yours
        since forever.
How can it be, How did you know me?
Wonderous ways, feel your gaze go right
        through me, eyes upon me
Awakening this
Gentle breeze?

What feelings i've had
when together in spirit Chanting
waves crashing against my heart in smooth
        decadence
decadence, pulsing, lifeblood, healing an eternity
noone could understand this, from where our
        hearts speak
or the constant love we could never begin to
        seek

feeling you on me, unabashedly Primal
can't tell you where i am but i am gone
Far away from this cold place
somewhere in the stars, Uncountable, reeling....
so in awe, so lost in feeling

hearing the wolf breathe
still silent, needs no words
bowled over with intensity, awash with a tidal
        wave

caressing me

now contented, at peace
spirit love release
You're a voice in the night
Awakening me
calls to me, i can sense your thoughts of me,
feeling me

Taking me, for I was always yours

Betrayal Mutual

How Can I Ever Explain?
trying to write this down
What you never gave me, the chance
to Verbalize, when you
installed those Eyes
to spy on me
never thought for one second you'd turn your
lies on Me

if you could recall for just one moment
how I could make you feel,
so much Love from one so Real, then maybe
        with
Time you could begin to grasp
what you have lost now.

You knew that my trust had eroded
With all of my love-lost, emoted
and in all my grief, I Tried my hand
at playing those at my Command

for when You arrived, you see
they were only amusement to me
I only wanted One, you know and it
Came so fast and we Fell so hard
Three weeks and i felt Together
We shared from deep inside
all the wounds in our lives
but of the two

only one held more hurt than I
and that one was You

as within that jaded heart love took a turn
and now this heart can beat no More
only unspoken anger abides
a vengeance was unleashed, the iceberg's tip
and as mistrust caused your spying down to
misperceived lying, so untrue
would our actions only serve to Protect
Perception, A betrayal Mutual

you and i

it took awhile for me to understand
just how did we find ourselves aching, so
simultaneously,
Victims of
some Others' interpretations of
Our own self- worths?

Throwing our cautions to the wind we Loved, so
        fiercely,
so unaware that more pain could befall
us, so naively trusting them....
Hadn't we had our fill?
Two hearts that burned cold long ago, yours and
        mine
Until two more came to singe them further

How odd to be thrown together sharing pain
        meant for one soul
Pain meant to be suffered alone
Torturous pain and resolve, resignation, ends to
        some means
We don't yet understand
Luck blessed us with a means to an end
    and it was
        you and i

A Human Doormat for your Soul

I thought we were beyond it all, thought that if
i could stand my ground we were ok
much to the chagrin of those who think we
    shouldn't
be friends
I thought that you'd made changes, yes,
that was what i would tell them
those issues shrinking to the back
good points emerging stronger
while some darkness remained, strongholds of
    your
Upbringing
things that beat you down that I thought you
    were
beginning to rise above and conquer
Wisdom coming with age and experience
Being used for good
Maturity emerging with a certain laid back grace
Self-actualization registering on your face

But when **She** comes back, Look out
Here comes the "trickle-down effect"
She mesmerizes you, changes you
Alters you, begins the heart atrophy
I can point to it and you can laugh
but we all know its true
She only makes an ass out of you
In your love for her you break, you bleed

in your search to find an aching need

Then unhappiness like that you've never known
Emerges turns your heart to stone
You eat, sleep and dream the pain, love flitting
       back and forth,
Pleasure to misery
You can no longer see
Tunnel vision emerges and the slightest spark
can evoke a combustion
So sudden and surprising that
no one can be sure what hit them
No fear of burning bridges there, the reason
       illogical,
Immaterial
to the naked eye or the average guy
But to hurt and not care and retaliate
Transferance undeserved
Were it to happen once more I'm fairly certain I
       am keeping score
And soon there will come a day when I can
       tolerate no more
For you have to understand this
That this dysfunctional relating is not the way it
       goes
Maybe you learned it that way, but Baby, it's
       time to grow
And the tears inside your head that you don't
       release
Might actually flow out in sweet , sweet release
Then those baby steps you've taken in standing
       up for thee
Won't come winging back , wounding the
       undeserving Me.

If you love me, you'll keep going
Take it as a compliment
From the one who saw you changing
when noone else wanted to see growth
When you said you loved me , you meant it
One day you might learn that those words do
      not mean
Verbal fists up
or that Someone is of
No use to you
Unless they become that
Human doormat for your soul.

BILLY

you could say that you never knew how much i
        cared
but that would never be true
a man like you, perceiver of truth, you stuff your
        deepest feelings
inside of you
and if someone were allowed to love you
as deeply as you need
An absolute concession
you would call it an Obsession
And bolt.

when your eyes met mine you tried to hide
to shield that little boy deep inside
that big boy softie everyone knows
with a few too many habits, sorta like my cat has
        toes
But I love that cat
and there's noone like him
he's a loyal cat
and he's in it for keeps
Which he may have a better way of showing

But
knowing you as i do
i may never get to the core of you
But its fairly comprehensive
and that means simple....
that even with your vices and your toys

and hanging with the boys
Bill remains someone to me
dear, true Harley blue

(that would be…) YOU

Ah…That Barry White voice with a twist…
how it just Goes Through Me
How can u affect me as you do already do?
i like to imagine your strong hands in a caress
You over me
Strength and passion taking hold
As I listen to your strong, even, full breaths
coming through the phone, I become lost in a
      race to
find myself asleep at your side
So craving your arms around me, and the
      indulgence of
hearing those very breaths come barreling
through your chest wall, engulfed in the very
      warmth of you
Desperate to know more of us and how we fit
      together
As I have experienced your making love to my
      mind
I can't help but wonder at the rest
Catching my breath with a certain smile

January 20, 2002

you 2

always thought you were
every woman's treasure
mister larger than life
could never measure
you

guiding me to new heights
wanting the best for me,
seeing my potential and my present good
Listen to you, I should
you've done it and seen it

wanting to keep me from needless harm
you always know just what to do
but now i dont know what to do with you

i once knew a man like you
who tried to tell me what to do
didn't do it the same way as you
but if you knew how i've always loved him
it would move mountains and
you

how i care runs deep
sometimes keeps me from my sleep for
i cannot spend time enough
those tender moments do you take them light
a kiss on the phone, giggling into the night?
You want a woman, smart and true

Be careful what you wish for
it could all turn on you

For in your striving
for those you love
to make and keep me whole
you may lose sight of your intent
and forget i have a soul

YOU-3

you don't know how angry you've made me
i don't really want to be banished from you
but i know how you work and i know i will be
         doing time
for this one

however short you will need cooling off
and time apart to blow off steam
you see, in your exasperation you will not see
that there is some hurt to be dealt with in me

im an old hand at a banter
i actually get a rise at hearing your voice raise
         above mine
in a crescendo sick as that may seem
but to know me you'd know where to stop

For you, one of the most caring men i know
when i couldnt trust another
might need to take a deep breath and know
that i need at least a brother
a pseudoincestuous mind melding brew
You and I, a Jew-Buh Catholic *Stew*
Admit it you jerk that I'm good for you

If you'd get off of that high horse you'd find
that the one who has had something made love
         to, her mind

thinks the World of the man who may have her
    by the balls
as she lets too much go, left and right
could never imagine us as anything but tight
conceding that nearly always youve been right
But when it comes to making me hurt,
Not
on this one!!

Finding Our Peace

how can you look away tonight
when the only thing crippling us is fear
knowing like you do of our marriage prior
a dream that just was, uninspired
the reality is, that you and i
came from a star known as We
Somewhere safe we were meant to be
but dreams get lost and misconstrued
lesions, paining from what people have done to
      you
and you may need to think because you've not
      known
a love in this life that could, in affect
Take you Home
where did we know it this love
remains to be seen
for until these eyes meet
those, honey we have never Been in love so true,
not this lifetime, so sweetheart look deep inside
      of you
and find your queen, your partner, your dream
rationality logic don't trade places with destiny
      or fate
if happiness is to be ours, we must recognize one
      another
before it feels as though it's too late
for the window is narrow for us to jump
      through

hand in hand together may be the only way for
us to
Reunite and finally find our Peace.

Sarah L. Brinklow

For you, When You Cared

You….who Are warm sun and starshine
summer winds and rain
if i couldn't sort my way through it all
fog lifted, you, again

How you have always seen the hurt
Often wished away my pain
were angered with the careless
state my heart found itself in

for you who yourself knew the agony and ache
tried to keep me oh so safe
hated So to stand back and watch
while all he did was Take

loverays

when all around me people snap
and i go so far as to question my own sanity and
     validity in recourse
i see you smile across the room inside my head
and i know i'm alright
because when they all fail me
You remain
steadfast and true
you've never shown anger
or gotten in my face, no nothing but LoveRays
shining all over the place
the warmth intensifying till the day i see you
i just can't explain it, just wanna be near you
you have a serenity no one can surpass, your wit
     and your humor damn it kicks ass
Sweet sweet man do you know what you bring
Warmth and joy to my heart and a safeness that
     sings rounds in my head lets me know Im
     not dead Im a child in
the light on that dark stormy night and you're
     there in my arms, hiding safe from the
     storms, to know you is to crave
More, and I know this, intuitively
that you and i go way back
there's such balance and symmetry.
I never want to be away from you in away that
     breaks a soul tie
Feelings endless, surprise us, a bond that need
     never die.

Bared

It would feel like forever
When hours and hours
Would feel like days
In you would walk, clearing that haze
That would become my thought calliope,
Circles, circles Blinding me
Weakness, the Big Picture, case in
Point
Whirlwind, Tidalwave
Cause a release from this joint
Pyramids, fear abating
The top, my reality
The bottom, dreams Unfulfilled
Representative of
A Life Stood still
Wheels turning, mind-a-whirring
Rear wheels spinning wildly
In that Rut, Rocking
Us free a bit too hard,
The danger being the precipice and the drop
     below
With myself yet alone at the wheel
It's a wonder that I can yet feel
My hope, should you be so inclined
Is that you could wind up inside
My mind, the crap you've seen me through
I thought time had bared my soul to you

YOU, 4....

Can't be sure I ever really knew
a man quite like you..
Forever looking out
beyond a shadow of a doubt
Once Misconstrued Control
for urging awake This Soul
when your agitation at times perceived
wrongly could have gotten the better of me
In the course of a day I could sit back and see,
Eventually
Just how deeply you cared for me
It's a rare combination, being cared for and
      driven,
Ridden hard
there were many times in life
i just couldn't see that as Living and would Run
with my tail between my legs, straight into some
      pit that could
Swallow me up
Whole.
My Natural Rebellion
does not want to know
that You could be Right
that it's not about Control
much rather run off into the night alone
      sometimes
Rather than take that Right Path
unsure what i might find.

That arms around me could affect this state of
    Mind
for we never know
that at the end of that tunnel
We could find the Light or
a Barreling Train
Contentment in the rays or
merely more Pain
Sometimes i find it hard to believe, somewhat
    difficult to
Perceive
that the taking of that Risk could make it all
    worth
the gamble of Living again
But with a gentle lover like you,
sweet Friend, so True
You could only seek to help me Strive
Empowering me to stay alive
in the healthiest of ways,lengthening my days
For you've shown me all the good you see
That pain has buried deep so deep inside of me
Contrasting hues of dark and light
Rays of Gold fade into night
Emparting faith and energy
to the trees, waving tall, a powerful breeze
for out of love and concern,
the Phoenix, she now can rise
out of these ashes,
Smoldering, never to burn

from the little girl

You open your Masterful arms, I run to them,
this frightened little girl who has only known
    fear
Will you abandon me when i block
it all, throw it aside in exchange for hopes and
    dreams
shooting for and craving
Total trust
The laugh of a Real man
head thrown back, unassuming
i want to believe i can devote myself to You
Great arms around me, all-encompassing
Romantic love, submission I never knew
Dashing fears to the ground
Beating swords into plowshares
we two
Something we've never been able to keep
Arms around us when we sleep
i've never known a man like you
that could make me feel contented at the
    thought
tied to a headboard arms around me
Yes to anything just do not harm me
Your collar, your mark, my surrender
my Submission
why?
because you taught this little girl to fly
In a cage of Love with an open door.

Chapter Four: Angst

The Day the Burqah Fell

Was it in exchange for
innocent souls
The day the Burqah fell?

And in your flag-waving arrogance
did you think that I could only
mean those
with the faces that
looked just like yours?
Unsuspected, incapsulated
the incinerated

Or could I perhaps have meant others
Those whose numbers will not be ascertained
By a Corporate News Network
or an American Broadcasting Company?
In camps riddled with disease
Those thousands of dead with brown faces?

Was it in the name of women
The day the Burqah fell?
Or can we, in realistic horror,
Greed bearing the masks of the dieties
For the day the Burqah fell
Our morals took that plunge to hell
We all became hypocrites, united that day
on opposing fronts
A "justifiable" Armageddon?

Was it all really committed for the women of
    Kabul
(The women who are not allowed to take in a
    show)
The day the Burqah fell?
Who are we, in fact, impressing
when the puppet son named
the reason for the hate Someone else's Jealousy
and the bullying Response
(otherwise known as "Resolve")
The day the Burqah fell
Jesus and Allah traded tears
Heads hung in shame
at their Spawn

Manhattan, 4 1/2 Months after the Fact

Manhattan, 4 1/2 months after the fact
Tens of thousands trampling the Apple
Fears shelved, heart-stirring emotion
saying No to the corporate rulers who
dine on shrimp cocktails while we stand
arm to arm, Corraled by the boys and girls in
     blue
(stressed beyond measure)
part of our New Military they were, they Are
Someone's pawns in a great, ugly game

Antagonistic? Who?
Them or us, hard to say?
or was it We?
On the edge, enforced misery
They lost brothers, sisters too
but if we really want to talk all-encompassing
     loss
liberties are next...........
I did not want to lose any of you!
The pain in your hearts I never knew
All those faces, young and vibrant
Our brightest and best taken down
In an act on our shores we have never known
     before

We all paint the bullseye
in red, blue and white

On those brown faces, axis of Evil
but as we do
Point that finger inward
at myself, me and you
For there are white faces equally accountable
We'd all be in true mourning if
we knew
That this great land might indeed possess
an internal enemy or two
Unfathomable as it may seem
Someone may hold a different dream.
Thinking as I do, my heart how it bleeds
for all of You
who
blew away on that
dark September day
And that fine dust that spread across that island
     Manhattan
now carries you all in the wind

Walking in your streets, Manhattan
and looking at my feet
bearing the Swoosh
(put there by brothers and sisters half a world
     away,
Ruled by the Iron fist of Greed in their direst
     need)
I noticed the dust on my once white symbols
of First World status.
A thought ensued,
and upon returning home, well
I just couldn't do it
I could not wash them, not ever. I cried!
As what they mean to me now

Possesses a far louder voice than new white
     shoes
What they mean to me now is
brothers and sisters
Half a world away, Working for dirt into the
     night
and those once alive!
Vibrant
Beautiful faces we cannot forget, for they were
Our
American Dream, Vaporized
Blasted so far into the Light

Six Months

They came back as two blue ghosts
delivering you to the stars
But you were already there, its just that we
      needed
closure
They had nothing to bury
Only pieces of you, had faded
memories, still fresh and pungent
Swirling all about us
particles we cannot see
Six months along, hanging in the air, a certain
Tension, there you live on the face of a cop,
Memorialized in forever-furrowed brows
That walk through Manhattan
with hair gone gray far too quickly

Glad We Never Met

Though I never listened to her
when the questions were raised
it seemed you didnt measure up,
werent good enough

Why couldn't I just see
that you were using me
a means unto your own
yet another one to bone

Thought I'd seen past all your crap
Saw a depth they didnt see
What the hell was I looking at
The only fool here is me

You see, I had it in my head
That you were caring, some kind of lover
I thought you thought so much of me
Now, it seems youd rather have my brother.

For the only head you've ever used
Is at the end of your tool
With all the things that you have fucked

You've broken every rule.
And to think I thought that waz cool.

RINGS

i could write about all sorts of things
but this time the subject material is rings
I've been in a quandry regarding this matter
So bear with me now while I discuss the latter

I've a ring from the school I attended as a girl
that was stepped on was it deliberately
I once owned a pearl
purchased by proxy by a prison pen pal
perhaps it was stolen back when they let him out
     of that jail.

Got a ring my mother got as a gift from my
     grandmother
she had the ring made with a cracked diamond
     center
once the tieclip of the man who helped conceive
     her and leave her
A lot of heartache in that ring
One now wonders if they truly are signs of
     eternal love or
betrayal?

when taking the plunge and saying i do
got a ring with a chip from the drunk who knew
that hed pawned it while i worked, in essence,
     telling me to screw
the beer meant far more than the commitment
At the time , who knew?

At one point I marvelled at the freedom of
          women
who still wear the rings, giving empty glances to
          their hands, no
Retrospect indulged these Cretinous givers
Comparable to notches on a belt
Being beyond me that nothing is felt....

Got a box full of promises
A box full of lies
I lie awake at night wondering how id despise
Wearing them all, each on a finger
I Wonder, in living , would I often linger
and drop everything with a look at a ring
Given as a pledge of an eternal thing
that died once upon a time
But in doing this, Do i cling?

I Killed You In My Mind Tonight

I killed you in my mind tonight
Somewhere between
the Bellowing and
the condescending blows
that shot through the receiver
ricocheting off the walls
of an Inner Ear gone numb
Long ago.

Falling backwards (not stepping)
down a step off that pedestal
You the Goodhearted
(another Empathetic Wonder)
set off alarms reverberating
Wildly
triggers abounding, mildly
the Understated
shaking me Awake
Reminding me
Never to make the Same Mistake

Valentine's Day

You
open the newspaper ads
bowled over by hearts,
Knowing otherwise, Yet running
a finger anyway down long columns,
Alphabetized
finding your name only followed
by a different initial

Another year
God, you can't take away this misery
from me!
Sadomasochistic dreaded
indulgence-avoidance
Someone picked the perfect month
Frozen February
dead, loveless.
Useless holiday from
Hell.

What the hell were
they thinking when they
Blew up all those hearts?
Craving an Uzi for a shopping trip
in my mind, deviously playing
target practice with
the
Bobbing hearts.

No one ever bought me one but once and
I was beaten that night so
I don't even count it
Everyone said "He's not so bad"
They couldn't see
and neither can any of you

Fraudulent acts of love
Expressly bought
for purposes malicious
Guilt, duty, payment
for services to be
Rendered

Call it what you will

But Valentines
are no more than
tokens paid to unknowing
Prostitutes.

So you can take your
Pink hearts and
Red panties
and Shove them where the sun don't shine

I'm making it a new
holiday in my mind
A day for Innocents
let them learn
to love the right way
Not burn or be burned

Paperbbag mailboxes

Sarah L. Brinklow

covered in hearts
Where everyone receives
abeit a World Unrealistic
Waxing Prolific
As we are all that
Little girl or boy
white knuckled
Tightly clutching that
Bag of Hearts.

Eggshells

A new man
knowing its not a mistake
a new love
So true, so not wanting my heart to ache
for the thought of going it again, well
Time says its just a chance I have to Take,
As it may take some getting used to
not walking on eggshells,
fearing they might break

Blame

its not clear to me
why a man's moods have a woman to blame
at their helm, why
it was probably joan of arc's own fault that she
    was burned
but never peter's or paul's why they're gone
that if you hadn't done A (so what if it was by
    mistake?)
that B would have never occurred so
Leave it
Drop it
Just Stop it
Say no more
treat me like I am your whore
here for yor convenience
Drop me, Stop me, Gag me,
Subdue
For none of our feelings could ever be true
Our sole purpose (allegedly) serving you.
For a woman and a bad Master
Is a recipe for disaster
You can't expect her not to slip
In a dominant relationship
if love and respect don't go hand in hand
with that dick in my face and my head in your
    hands
you can't expect phallic worship without
    adoring me

Like Flaming Fields Stoked by a Gentle Breeze

one day you will have used enough of us, maybe
    then
you'll see
that you took a piece of me

Does Anyone Give?

do any of us really
give a flying fuck about the other?
(just wondered)

i used to, he whispered on the chat rat
        till i got sick of bein fucked over....

people searching, paining futility
        Painting futility
Come for me
    Clean my surface filth, bathe me in caresses
        Take away my pain. God take it away.
Please what do i have to do?
Can you hold me, take it away, take me away
please, i beg it of you
Hold me in your heart
we must never part
For i've parted enouugh
and i have seen it all
been through the shit
all of it, all
Dont want to hurt no more, take the pain away,
        please,
i'm
down on my knees
why can't any one see
or care to the bottom of me
u see, i've put forth the work,

Like Flaming Fields Stoked by a Gentle Breeze

i've given it my all, yet
i've stilll come up
Emptyhanded

Does anyone even have
a fuckin clue
whats gone on in side of you
when you say u hurt, u bleed
And noone sees a flying fuck
i want to drive you to your knees, crying oh my
            fucking God
Why didn't i see?

Why didn't i see
what was going on
inside of me
what went on, inside of you, Unnoticed?

my eyes are closed, i can no longer see
you
take me from pain
37 hail marys and can i be better
locked in a cyclical poverty parade
of sorts, you, unwilling as a gender, unscathed
as you go about your bidding, and I remain
            chained
In a role from which i could not break free
no one knows what indeed is inside of me

and you may never know unless we light
talk about into the night
see the things that alone might be seen
in moonlight, or was it in starlight, Lean

into me, oh don't leave me here, alone,
Apart, so devoid of fearless reciprocity
That burns and fuels. and fuels and voids
that fills the deep deep deep devoid
where they didn't belong but still you took
them from their shelves and gave them some
        semblance of
consciousness

You don't have a clue
what has happened to you
you don't know why i am what i am
Nor do i
My lover is me, You cannot fulfill me
No one will ever give me what can fuse me
together i want to be whole , come on use me
Make me feel spent, make me know what it feels
        to be
Woman and needed and not lived without

Don't give me any more room to be happy sad
        or doubt
Do you have a name in my stupor i need you
i cant even think what is it i need to
i can't love i can't feel my kidneys are seizing
i am not in a way that i feel good about
keep thinking that soon my whole lifeblood
        peters out
and then where will i be there's no one to my
        name and
i don't think that my kids will want much from
        this game so
Shut it just shut it unless you can love me

Like Flaming Fields Stoked by a Gentle Breeze

i
don't think that there is anyone out there for me
Complete me now
use me now
make me oh so yours
take me oh take me oh
anywhere on shores that i do not know will not
        know cannot feel will not know
feel like my life will seep from me and you will
        not
notice and life
will lie fleeting and i will be no more than a drop
        in the
Proverbial buck it
i'm drunk so i
love you
and what's up but fuck it!!!!

penis envy

oh please, save me all of your whining
you're really no different than the rest
you have limitations marinating in testosterone
you demand all my attention but soon you are
Smothered!

i am an individual
you cannot own me
i've heard it time and time again
you cannot tell me what to do

You are not putting out enough
…do you even swallow? (i do)
You don't even like my friends
(the tirades vary widely ,dependent on the
        decade of the
Model)

What do you need that much money for?
I Said, for the fifth time, do I have to repeat?
It doesn't matter!!
No, leave it!!

Are you really gonna wear that?
God, how long does it take you?
Aren't you getting a little fat?
You're starting to sound just like your mother !
Are are you on the rag or what?

Like Flaming Fields Stoked by a Gentle Breeze

Be my priest at the pulpit
my daddy in bed
overemphasizing the importance of whether I
        give head
try to walk me over hot coals
send me to work but expect a hot meal
while performing a white glove test
(and call That multitasking!!)

You can take all your Hirsuite talk
Beat your chest and swing from vines
March into war and justify it
patrolling the universe, weapon in your hip
        holster
but on second thought , why don't you

Live in a cage in the corner of an Amazon cave
speak when your spoken to
it's only when you're a good boy that you'll get
        head
on third thought, Roll over, bitch, play dead.
the only way you'll get a piece of me
is after i
Cost you half the humiliation
that your fucking gender has cost me
blacken your eyes and give it the knee
Tie that pussy boy body to the nearest tree
and give you what I'M after
so Bend Over.

A sense of satisfaction of the first degree
the only good man is the man who learns
        humility
and knows who is in control

knows how to give up their very soul
and keep it there, maintaining a state of grace
Giving honour to the ones who put you in
This Fucking Place.

Castaway Sarah

now on that island known as personal numbness
throbbing native drums coarsing through my
      veins
i cant help but feel spent
Exhausted , for after love lost, each stealing a
      chunk of
Soul matter
not sure what they've left not sure what they've
      broken
talk to me and listen hard, for when i defeat
      myself before you've had
that chance, should it perplex you, it's an old
      trick i learned long ago
to keep my guard up
Head swirling, brain burning
Up to here in knee deep shit of the mental sort
Read the report, wake up and smell the
      proverbial coffee, misunderstood
though thought self pretty direct,
Penile emoteddd, sorry Freudian typo
Little girl underlying
only looking under the sofa for the pieces to fit
      her little puzzle
God fucking help you if you take advantage of
      her back being turned.

castaway sarah
curled up in a ball
in her red flannel gown on the floor, exhausted

washed up on the shores of a great fairy tale or
      two
that very nearly involved
You.

Who Knows Where the Time Goes

Who knows where the time goes, who knows
    where the love flows
who knows how the little ones we carry grow till
    we have to look up
to see their eyes when it used to be looking
    down in our arms
Who knows when love is no more, when the
    walls of your heart hold a revolving door..
Dreams cast in memory, love has no end
how many bridges have burned, fair lover, true
    friend
In the course of a lifetime from the first cry and
    the soul leaving the sky
to the time we lie still and It comes for us, and it
    will come for us all
I have to say many, many will have loved, and
    lost
But those ties, they bind in heart and mind
and when that last breath is to be breathed
and you find yourself clutching your chest on
    the other side of the globe in a city far
    away
if you can't be here still to hold my hand and
    whisper it to me
then mouth these few words "i love you now
    break free"
you see, that would mean so much to me
for years of silence will have wounded me

and impaired my happiness , a fight i would
      have had to lead
Say that you loved me, let me hear it on winds
      blowing through
This desolate heart that was true to you
And this gentle breeze will return once more
To give you what you were once looking for.

About the Author

Sarah Brinklow is a writer of poetry, fiction, and has contributed work to various independent news websites as well as local news publications. Originally from Penfield, New York, she has a B.S in English from the State University of New York College at Brockport. Her loves and travels to them have taken her to the United Kingdom Her two children, John and Casey, are the future, who are the only ones who truly will ever count to her on this adventure known as Life.

0-595-22041-X